T0131608

Peanut Power

Welcome to Your
Peanut Power Journey

Avril Ann Lochhead

Illustrations by David Lochhead

BALBOA.
PRESS
A DIVISION OF HAY HOUSE

Balboa Press books may be ordered through booksellers or by contacting:

Balboa Press
A Division of Hay House
1663 Liberty Drive
Bloomington, IN 47403
www.balboapress.com.au
1 (877) 407-4847

Print information available on the last page.

ISBN: 978-1-5043-1083-3 (sc)
ISBN: 978-1-5043-1084-0 (e)

Balboa Press rev. date: 11/17/2017

*Further food for thought to
continue your journey to freedom*

More Peanut Power

and

Another Taste of Peanut Power

When very young, an elephant is tied to a short rope fastened to a stake in the ground.

This trains the elephant to stay within the limitations of the immediate area.

Even when fully grown, the elephant is not aware that freedom is there for the taking.

We, like the elephant, have been conditioned.

Our habitual attitudes, thoughts, and even feelings can immobilise us.

Our thoughts are our most powerful tools and fuel of creation.

We can use them negatively, or as suggested in this offering of peanuts, we can tap into our potential, unlimited greatness.

Add these peanuts to your daily diet, and move in the direction of your dreams.

Allow them to enrich your experience of living, loving, and embrace your magnificence.

Have fun and play with these peanuts of thought.

Follow their trail to freedom.

Attitude

everything really begins
and ends with this.
You make your experience of life either
heaven or hell.

You choose!

This page is for you to open your peanut.

Your thoughts.

Your feelings.

Next steps.

Bliss

every moment, everywhere—whether gardening,
closing an amazing deal, or ironing.
Wonder full.

This page is for you to open your peanut.

Your thoughts.

Your feelings.

Next steps.

Compassion

firstly, for yourself and then for others.

You will experience a certain ease in life.

This page is for you to open your peanut.

Your thoughts.

Your feelings.

Next steps.

$\mathcal{D}$iscovery

is the most exciting past-time as it creates your future, in who you are being right now!

Observing, noticing, choosing direction, action, learning.

It is so exciting!

This page is for you to open your peanut.

Your thoughts.

Your feelings.

Next steps.

*E*nergy

is often what you are most keenly aware
of when you don't have enough.

When you have energy, you don't even think to
stop for lunch, because you are so engrossed and
engaged in your delicious life.

This page is for you to open your peanut.

Your thoughts.

Your feelings.

Next steps.

*F*eelings

are to be embraced, acknowledged,
and appreciated.

Allow them to guide you gently.

This page is for you to open your peanut.

Your thoughts.

Your feelings.

Next steps.

Generosity

like charity; begins at home,
not only with money.

Speak generously to yourself;
praise each step on your way.

You will then generate more
generosity for others.

This page is for you to open your peanut.

Your thoughts.

Your feelings.

Next steps.

*H*andle it now!

End procrastination and suffering.

If something is on your mind, get informed.

Pick a course of action, take 1 step and move forward, or move it out of your space.

Make this a practice, and watch life get simpler and simpler.

This page is for you to open your peanut.

Your thoughts.

Your feelings.

Next steps.

Intuition

needs your attention; or more correctly,
you need to listen to your "in"tuition.

Inner guidance is always ready when you are.

This page is for you to open your peanut.

Your thoughts.

Your feelings.

Next steps.

Journeying

through life is unpredictable.

Learn how to go with the flow.
Build bridges when necessary,
or erect dams if required.

You will need at least to be willing
not to know and to listen.

This page is for you to open your peanut.

Your thoughts.

Your feelings.

Next steps.

*K*indle

your self-esteem; make lots of appreciative deposits.

Gently add more acceptance for being exactly the way you are.

Change what you choose when you are ready.

This page is for you to open your peanut.

Your thoughts.

Your feelings.

Next steps.

*L*iveliness

is expressing your passion and experiencing life fully in each moment.

Share the risk and joy with others.

This page is for you to open your peanut.

Your thoughts.

Your feelings.

Next steps.

Manage

your circumstances, and you will have peace on earth.

Ignore or dominate them, and you will have hell to pay.

Nothing can change if you don't.

This page is for you to open your peanut.

Your thoughts.

Your feelings.

Next steps.

Natural

with ease and grace.

There is nothing so refreshing as someone who clearly hasn't got it all handled and yet is inspired by the challenge.

This page is for you to open your peanut.

Your thoughts.

Your feelings.

Next steps.

Openness

is the way to stop using energy, protecting stuff.

If you have any skeletons, embrace them if you can.

You need to be at home with your past.

This page is for you to open your peanut.

Your thoughts.

Your feelings.

Next steps.

*P*resence

is being quietly productive,
extraordinarily competent,
and excruciatingly effective—easily.

This page is for you to open your peanut.

Your thoughts.

Your feelings.

Next steps.

Quiet

time is the most important access to creativity.

Pathways to be considered, actions to be taken,

other avenues of action not previously heard.

This page is for you to open your peanut.

Your thoughts.

Your feelings.

Next steps.

Role

playing is at epidemic proportions
on the way to getting somewhere.

Check that you consciously design and
choose the somewhere you are heading.

Make sure that it is somewhere you really
want to go, and you are someone you really
want to be.

This page is for you to open your peanut.

Your thoughts.

Your feelings.

Next steps.

*S*urrender

is challenging your boundaries.

Going beyond what is predictable.

Allowing fear and not letting it stop you.

Trusting in yourself and the process,
knowing that you can succeed!

This page is for you to open your peanut.

Your thoughts.

Your feelings.

Next steps.

$\mathcal{T}$rusting

is something beyond and yet inside.

A flow of knowing you're on course,
especially when there is no evidence.

That takes courage, too.

This page is for you to open your peanut.

Your thoughts.

Your feelings.

Next steps.

*U*niversal

interconnectedness would eliminate our
sense of separation.

We all have similar deep concerns.

Practice listening for the gold,
the juice in your relationships.

You will know when you tap in.
All distance will disappear.

It's better than winning the lottery!

This page is for you to open your peanut.

Your thoughts.

Your feelings.

Next steps.

Values

are important.
Are yours really yours?

Did you inherit them?

If so, you are not stuck with them.

Challenge and choose your own.
Then walk your talk!

This page is for you to open your peanut.

Your thoughts.

Your feelings.

Next steps.

*W*illingness

to love and be loved.

This is a leap of faith.

Are you worthy of loving and being loved?

Yes! Definitely.

This page is for you to open your peanut.

Your thoughts.

Your feelings.

Next steps.

X-Ray

is seeing, hearing, and relating to more than is obvious.

Relate to your own and their magnificence.

Be xtraxtra-loving.

This page is for you to open your peanut.

Your thoughts.

Your feelings.

Next steps.

$\mathcal{Y}$outhfulness

is keeping the wonder alive.

Make life a game worth playing.

Watch children play and learn; they
have this one handled.

This page is for you to open your peanut.

Your thoughts.

Your feelings.

Next steps.

Zen

is the art of living peacefully, harmoniously, and lovingly in a world that may constantly challenge you.

Harmony will begin where you are.

This page is for you to open your peanut.

Your thoughts.

Your feelings.

Next steps.

About the author

Avril Ann Lochhead is an enthusiastic and visionary trainer, whose results in personal empowerment are an unqualified success.

As a transitional specialist, Avril believes we can go beyond our previous thinking to access new levels of fulfilment we desire for ourselves, our families and our communities.

Embracing current circumstances, trusting an internal feeling of respect and esteem for your "Self", are the fundamental ingredients of being fulfilled.

When this relationship with yourself is regained and fully expressed, you can then expand - and offer your contribution, generosity and appreciation to others.

Your life takes on a truly magnificent flavour.

May all your peanuts be positive!

Printed in the United States
By Bookmasters